IMAGES
of America

MORVEN

This photograph shows Morven's wisteria in its full glory. Notice the additional trellises trailing it up to the second floor. When the Princeton Garden Club hosted a tour of the town's gardens in 1926, Morven's wisteria proved to be the site's chief attraction. (Courtesy of Morven Archive.)

ON THE COVER: Pres. Warren G. Harding is pictured with the Stockton family on the day of the Princeton Battle Monument dedication in 1922. (Collection of the Historical Society of Princeton.)

IMAGES
of America

MORVEN

Elizabeth Allan and Jesse Gordon Simons

ARCADIA
PUBLISHING

Published by Arcadia Publishing
Charleston, South Carolina

Printed in the United States of America

Library of Congress Control Number: 2023940711

For all general information, please contact Arcadia Publishing:
Telephone 843-853-2070
Fax 843-853-0044
E-mail sales@arcadiapublishing.com

Visit us on the Internet at www.arcadiapublishing.com

This book is dedicated to Constance M. Greiff and Wanda S. Gunning, whose incredible documentation of Morven's history makes our work possible every day.

CONTENTS

ACKNOWLEDGMENTS

On behalf of Morven Museum & Garden, we would like to thank those who came before us in preserving and documenting this historic site. Any student of Princeton history stands on the shoulders of Constance Greiff and Wanda Gunning, whose incredible scholarship has uncovered centuries of local history. Morven was particularly fortunate to be the subject of their 2004 book *Morven: Memory, Myth, and Reality*, without which this publication would not exist.

The New Jersey Historical Society and the New Jersey State Museum stewarded the museum in the post-governor years. Countless historians, horticulturists, preservationists, and archaeologists ensured that Morven would stand into the 21st century and beyond. Historic Morven, Inc., was formed in 1987 as a friends group to support the creation of a freestanding organization with Georgia Schley leading the nascent years, opening the National Historic Landmark as Morven Museum & Garden in 2004. We also thank the generations of Morven docents who have welcomed visitors and brought history to life for decades.

Tireless dedication by Morven staff was vital to the success of the project, especially our executive director, Jill Barry, and curator of education, Greer Luce, who read every word of this book. Thanks in advance to Kathy O'Hara, who will carry this book in Morven's much-lauded Museum Shop. Curatorial interns Meredith Boyle, Bridget Casey, and Stefanie Taylor provided excellent assistance with this project in gathering information and images.

Many institutions in New Jersey and beyond provided documents and photographs for this project. Thank you to Princeton University Library, Special Collections at Princeton Theological Seminary, the New Jersey State Museum, Independence Hall National Historical Park, the Library of Congress, Princeton University Art Museum, and the National Library of Scotland. Special thanks are due to Stephanie Schwartz, curator of Collections and Research at the Historical Society of Princeton, who assisted with dozens of images for this publication. Finally, thank you to the families of those who called Morven home. Stocktons, Johnsons, and the children of many governors have generously shared their memories and photographs, allowing Morven's history to come to life.

INTRODUCTION

As Morven Museum & Garden embarks on its 20th year of operating as a museum in 2024, this book takes the opportunity to commemorate the many chapters of Morven's past. Located in Princeton, New Jersey, Morven has stood witness to 265 years of history. The land on which Morven sits is part of Lenapehoking, the ancestral homeland of the Lenni-Lenape people. King's Highway, or Stockton Street, which runs directly in front of Morven, connecting Trenton to New Brunswick, was first a pathway created by the Lenni-Lenape. In 1701, William Penn granted several thousand acres of land to Richard Stockton (c. 1652–1709). The land passed to his son John Stockton and was then given to his son Richard Stockton, "the Signer," who had a home built on the site around 1757.

Morven's appearance and footprint have changed over the centuries as fire and varying additions left their mark. Incredibly, Morven remained in one family from the 1750s into the 1940s. The Stocktons were often on the national and even international scene, starting with Richard Stockton, a signer of the Declaration of Independence. As wealthy lawyers, the first two generations of Stocktons at Morven enslaved men, women, and children on site. The Stocktons lived a comfortable lifestyle and increased their wealth through the forced labor of enslaved people. Like other signers of the Declaration of Independence, Richard Stockton did not seem to struggle with the inconsistency of holding people in bondage while signing a document that declared "that all men are created equal, that they are endowed by their Creator with certain unalienable Rights, that among these are Life, Liberty and the pursuit of Happiness." The rhetoric of revolutionary America—freedom, equality, and liberty—was inescapably intertwined with the practice of slavery.

After the Gradual Abolition Act of 1804, enslaved labor was replaced at Morven by paid servants. The domestic workforce was then made up of young women from Ireland and Germany. Physical traces of people working, whether enslaved or free, at Morven in the early years are hard to come by. They were not wealthy enough to have their portraits taken and were often left out of the historical record by those who documented it. Therefore, a reader of this book will not see a plethora of images of these people, but a committed effort to record more of their history is ongoing.

Morven has always been home to multigenerational groups stretching beyond the so-called nuclear family. It was almost always a bustling place, with the majority of families having more than six children—a statistic that held true throughout the governors' era. Grandparents, aunts and uncles, and cousins often came to stay. In the 1880s, Samuel Witham Stockton created an apartment within Morven's East Wing for his brother-in-law Archibald Alexander Hodge, his wife, Margaret, and their twin girls, nicknamed Bini and Bibi, to live alongside his family of nine. Additionally, Stockton fathers frequently used their land and wealth to build homes for their children and their families, creating a Princeton landscape that still exists today.

In this book, we include photographs of other Stockton properties in an effort to present a fuller picture of the community at each point in history.

The centennial of the signing of the Declaration of Independence in 1876 and then of George Washington's death in 1899 set off the Colonial Revival movement in the United States, making all things Colonial the latest craze. Helen Stockton rose to the occasion, celebrating Morven's revolutionary history and promoting her home alongside the founding fathers' most famous seats like Mount Vernon and Monticello. She spent decades restoring Morven and its gardens to the colonial era, embellishing its history along the way and leaving webs of myths for historians to unravel later.

As Helen Stockton aged, the upkeep of a large historic estate was a burden, and she therefore leased the property to captain of industry Robert Wood Johnson Jr. and his new wife, Margaret Shea. Moving in with their young daughter Sheila, they left their own mark on the property by adding a wonderful Art Moderne pool and pool house. Helen ultimately protected Morven's future by selling it to Gov. Walter Edge and his wife, Camilla, with the understanding that the home remain the governor's mansion or a public historic site, securing its legacy as an important piece of American history.

Beginning with Walter and Camilla Edge, Morven took on a new role as the official home of the New Jersey governor. As such, it hosted conversations between political leaders and its inhabitants as history continued to unfold. In 1954, Edge transferred Morven to the State of New Jersey. Honoring the requirements of Helen Stockton, Walter Edge then set up the deed to the state that would ensure Morven's future.

Gov. Robert Meyner followed the Edges, and soon Morven was run by a full-time staff of secretaries, state police, cooks, and housekeepers. Architectural changes were made to accommodate modern families, and the house took on a public role as New Jersey's home. After the Meyners, three more governors and their families lived at Morven: Richard Hughes, William Cahill, and Brendan Byrne. Despite being a grand historic home, it was too small to truly function as a governor's mansion. With public and private space being one and the same, First Lady Elizabeth Hughes had been said to cheerfully command her children ahead of any event, "Get dressed or get out." Governor Byrne and his family became the last to call Morven home when it was decided that Drumthwacket would better serve as the executive mansion.

With Walter Edge's proviso, Morven was then turned into a historical museum. First run as an adjunct site by the New Jersey Historical Society, then the New Jersey State Museum, it underwent a battery of interior and exterior renovations. In October 2004, Morven Museum & Garden opened to the public. For nearly 20 years, the museum has been open to visitors, celebrating the history of the site complemented by more than 30 special exhibitions showcasing the cultural heritage of the state.

Greiff and Gunning said it best when they wrote, "Morven has survived war, fire, changing tastes, the wear and tear of long occupancy, and varied uses. Yet throughout its long history, it has steadily provided visitors with a link to the past." It is our hope this collection of images provides a window into our shared history through the lens of this special home.

One

RICHARD AND ANNIS BOUDINOT STOCKTON

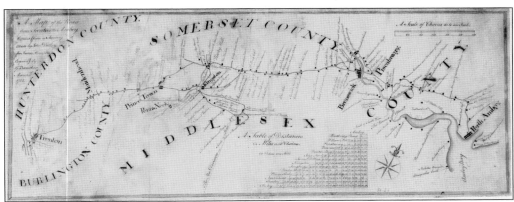

In 1701, Richard Stockton (c. 1652–1709), known as "the Settler," purchased the land on which Morven would stand from William Penn (1644–1718) for £900. The deed conveyed 5,500 acres, which contained portions of today's Mercer, Middlesex, and Somerset Counties. In 1762, John Dalley drew "A Map of the Road from Trenton to Amboy." Visible is the property of Richard's grandson, Richard Stockton, Esq. ("the Signer"). (Courtesy of Collection of Princeton University Library.)

The Barracks was built in 1684 and was only the second Colonial house in town. Richard Stockton (c. 1652–1709) and his wife, Susannah Witham Robinson (1668–1749), rented and eventually bought the home; their son John and his wife, Abigail, also lived here, and their son, Richard Stockton, the Signer, was presumably born here. Rose Studio captured the building as it was in 1904. (Courtesy of the Historical Society of Princeton.)

This meetinghouse of the Society of Friends, shown here around 1900, was built in 1759 after the 1724 structure burned. Although Richard Stockton was not a practicing Quaker, he is buried in the graveyard. As was the custom with many Quakers, those at Stony Brook did not mark their graves, so the precise site of his burial is unknown. This building still stands today. (Courtesy of Collection of Historical Society of Princeton.)

Richard Stockton (1730–1781) was born in Princeton. He attended the College of New Jersey and graduated in its first class in 1748. Richard qualified as an attorney in 1754. His parents gifted him the Morven property around the same time. He married Annis Boudinot in 1757 or 1758. Although an advocate for liberty, the Signer reported enslaving three people in 1779 and two in 1780. (Courtesy of Morven Collection.)

Annis Boudinot Stockton (1736–1801), shown in this companion portrait, was one of the first women published in the colonies. When Congress temporarily moved to Princeton from Philadelphia in the summer of 1783, the widowed Annis hosted members of Congress, earning herself the nickname the "Muse of Morven." Annis dined at Gen. George Washington's quarters at Rocky Hill, and he made at least one stop at Morven. (Courtesy of Morven Collection.)

By the 1760s, Richard Stockton felt that the landholdings his family had amassed warranted the status of a gentleman and the right to a family coat of arms. Stockton wrote to a former student in England to help him procure this design, which was made into a bookplate. He instructed that "the motto be Omnia Deo pendent," which means "everything depends on God." (Courtesy of the Collection of the Princeton University Library.)

Annis Stockton is shown at about 60 years of age in this pastel by James Sharples Sr. (c. 1751–1811). Although Richard's will stipulated that she could live at Morven until her death, she handed the property over to her son Richard and his new bride, Mary Field Stockton. Annis died while visiting her daughter Abigail Stockton Field at White Hill, Bordentown, in 1801. (Courtesy of Collection of Independence National Historical Park.)

Richard Stockton was one of five New Jersey signers of the Declaration of Independence. Four months after signing, he was captured and imprisoned by the British. Almost a year after his release, Stockton appeared before New Jersey's Committee of Safety to swear an "Oath of Abjuration and Allegiance," renouncing his oath of allegiance to the king and swearing allegiance to the new government in New Jersey. (Courtesy of the National Archives.)

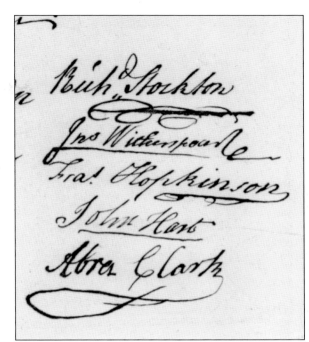

Richard Stockton, portrayed posthumously in this 1791 sketch by John Trumbull (1756–1843), was one of five signers of the Declaration of Independence to be captured during the war. He was imprisoned in Manhattan's Provost Jail, infamous for deplorable conditions, for about a month. Stockton lived another four years after release and died of cancer of the mouth in 1781. (Courtesy of Collection of Yale University Art Gallery. Gift of Mrs. Winchester Bennett.)

This is to certify that Marcus Marsh the bearer of this, was born at princeton in the state of new Jersey the first day of April 1765 in the family of Richard Stockton Esquire and since the decease of the said Richard Stockton the said Marcus has recieved his freedom from the widow of Richard Stockton who to this testimony sets her hand

Annis Stockton

Philadelphia
March the 2d 1798

Marcus Marsh was born into slavery at Morven on April 1, 1765. It appears that his mother died shortly thereafter or was sold by the Stocktons, as Annis Stockton served as Marcus's wet nurse. Upon Richard's death in 1781, Annis freed Marcus, and he went to live and work with Julia (Annis and Richard's daughter) and her husband, Benjamin Rush. Marcus worked alongside Dr. Rush as he battled the yellow fever epidemic in Philadelphia—staying by Rush's side when the doctor himself took ill. Rush wrote of Marcus, "I cannot tell you how much we all owe to Marcus. His integrity, industry, and fidelity deserve great praise." This record of manumission from 1798 was signed by Annis Stockton. Congress created this type of certificate to protect sailors from being impressed by the British navy. For African Americans, the certificate served as a way to officially document their freedom and was kept on their person at all times. (Courtesy of the collection of the National Archives, Proofs of Citizenship Used to Apply for Seamen's Certificates for the Port of Philadelphia, Pennsylvania.)

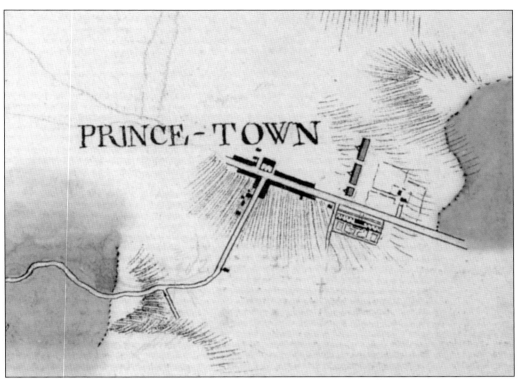

The detail of this 1781 map by Louis-Alexandre Berthier shows Morven and outlines of Annis Stockton's formal gardens at the time of Richard's death. The road running left to right is King's Highway (today's Stockton Street.) Morven is the structure visible along the bottom of the road with rectangular and L-shaped planting beds drawn behind the house. (Courtesy of Collection of Princeton University Library.)

Elias Boudinot IV (1740–1821), depicted here by Charles Wilson Peale, was the brother of Annis Stockton. He read law under Richard Stockton. Boudinot opened a law office in Elizabethtown, where he taught Alexander Hamilton. As president of the Continental Congress in 1782, he resided at Morven during the Congress's five-month stay in Princeton. (Courtesy of the Boudinot Collection of the Princeton University Art Museum. Gift of Mr. and Mrs. Landon K. Thorne.)

FINGAL,

AN

ANCIENT EPIC POEM,

In SIX BOOKS:

Together with several other POEMS, composed by

OSSIAN the Son of FINGAL.

Translated from the GALIC LANGUAGE,

By JAMES MACPHERSON,

Fortia facta patrum.   VIRGIL.

LONDON;
Printed for T. BECKET and P. A. De HONDT, in the Strand.
M DCC LXII.

The home of Richard and Annis suffered a serious fire on Christmas night 1758. They rebuilt the home and added a central block. Annis later christened the home Morven, meaning "big peak or mountain" in Gaelic. The name was taken from *Fingal: An Ancient Epic Poem in Six Books; Together with Several Other Poems, Composed by Ossian the Son of Fingal*, which was published in 1762. (Courtesy of the National Library of Scotland.)

This c. 1999 photograph shows Morven's West Wing, the oldest part of the structure, during restoration. With layers of limewash and paint removed, the earliest surviving construction of the West Wing was revealed. The infilled brick marks the location of the original smaller windows, reflecting the lower ceiling of the 18th-century building. (Courtesy of Morven Archive.)

Two

RICHARD AND MARY FIELD STOCKTON

Known as "the Duke" for his imperious manner, Richard Stockton (1764–1828) was the first son of Richard (the Signer) and Annis. He graduated from the College of New Jersey and became a lawyer like his father. This portrait by Christian Gullager shows him around 1800. He enslaved men, women, and children at Morven, including Thomas Jewell, Hannibal Simpson, Anthony ?, Batty ?, Catherine ?, Dinah ?, Fan ?, Nancy ?, Phillis ?, Sampson ?, and Susan ?. A question mark denotes that the last name is currently unknown to the authors. (Courtesy of Morven Collection.)

This companion portrait shows Mary Field Stockton (1766–1837) of Bordentown, who married the Duke in 1788. The Field and Stockton families were doubly related, as Mary's brother Robert wed Richard's sister Abigail. The couple moved into Morven with Annis Stockton. Letters indicate that the two women did not always get along. Mary and Richard raised nine children together. A number of love letters from her husband survive. (Courtesy of Morven Collection.)

This portrait by Charles B. Lawrence depicts the Duke in his later years. By 1820, he had served in both the Senate and House of Representatives and continued to run his successful law practice. The large classical column seen in the background highlights these distinguished professions. (Courtesy of Morven Collection.)

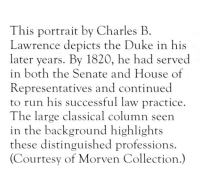

Like the companion portrait of her husband by Charles B. Lawrence, this portrait of Mary Field Stockton depicts her later in life. Richard and Mary made many changes to Morven, including the reconstruction of the entire center block of the house. The heights of ceilings and windows were increased, and semicircular fan lights were fitted over the front and rear doors. (Courtesy of Morven Collection.)

Mary Field Stockton grew up at Fieldsboro, also known as White Hill, in Bordentown, New Jersey. When her brother Robert married Richard Stockton's sister Abigail, the couple made the large mansion on the banks of the Delaware River their home. Robert Field greatly mismanaged the estate, and Richard Stockton provided loans to keep them afloat. When Robert Field died in 1810, Abigail returned to Princeton. (Courtesy of Library of Congress.)

After the death of Richard Field in 1810, the Duke built a home for his sister Abigail in Princeton called Rose Cottage. In 1917, it became Rose Cottage Tea House, which raised money for the American Fund for French Wounded and Red Cross during World War I. The building was torn down in 1960. (Courtesy of the Historical Society of Princeton.)

The Duke made many improvements to the Morven landscape. Perhaps his most lasting change was the planting of what is known as the Horse Chestnut Walk, which connected Morven's eastern entrance to present-day Bayard Lane. Visible in this photograph is another horse chestnut planted at the rear of the house. It survived for over a hundred years until it was felled by a storm in the 1920s. (Courtesy of Morven Collection.)

Richard Stockton was a trustee of the Presbyterian Church, and when the Princeton Theological Seminary was founded in 1812, the Duke donated about half of the land the seminary acquired. This drawing by Alexander Anderson (1775-1870) depicts the seminary's Alexander Hall in 1843. He was also the treasurer and then a trustee of the College of New Jersey (today Princeton University). The Duke took a harsh attitude toward students—standing by the expulsion of half of the student body after their petitions and protests for more personal liberty. His attitudes toward personal rights may be best summed up in his support for the Constitution but his disapproval of the amendments that make up the Bill of Rights. (Courtesy of Special Collections, Princeton Theological Seminary Library.)

In 1826, Richard Stockton, the Duke, gave his daughter Annis Stockton (1804–1842) and her husband, John Renshaw Thomson, land across Stockton Street. Their home, known as Thomson Hall, was designed by Charles Steadman. Thomson's second wife, Josephine Ward, added the mansard roof and bequeathed the home to Princeton. It served as a community center and then as Borough Hall until 1967. (Courtesy of the Historical Society of Princeton.)

These carved sphinxes and the large spheres in front of them once graced the front entrance of Thomson Hall. They are visible in the previous photograph (one sphere sits beneath the shrub by the steps). When the building was demolished in 1973, the sphinxes were moved to Morven's east entrance, where they still welcome visitors today. (Courtesy of Morven Archive.)

This building was originally the stable for Thomson Hall. In 1909, it was moved to 55 Mercer Street and remodeled for use as the Princeton Borough Hall from 1909 to 1936. It has since been used as a lending library, an American Legion post, and today as a Princeton Theological Seminary classroom. (Courtesy of the Historical Society of Princeton.)

This view from the southwest shows Morven in 1840. Visible is the front portico that was added in 1812. The Duke referred to it as "Mrs. S's portico," possibly because she is said to have paid for it from the sale of eggs and milk. In 1821, a fire caused damage to the central block, destroying the roof as well as many Stockton possessions. (Courtesy of the Historical Society of Princeton.)

Tusculum, seen here, was built for John Witherspoon, president of Princeton University and another signer of the Declaration of Independence, in 1773. In 1815, the Duke purchased the property, adding to his large landholdings in Princeton. Upon the Duke's death in 1828, the home passed to his son Samuel Witham Stockton (1801–1836), who lived there until his death eight years later. (Courtesy of the Historical Society of Princeton.)

Another improvement made by the Duke was the construction of an icehouse in this period. Built of stone, its vaulted ceiling, visible here in the 1990s, rises four and a half feet above ground. The double walls taper toward a stone floor, which is ten and a half feet below grade. The ice stored here was likely harvested from a pond on the Morven property. (Courtesy of Morven Archive.)

Three

ROBERT FIELD AND HARRIET POTTER STOCKTON

Robert Field Stockton (1795–1866), was the son of Richard (the Duke) and Mary Stockton. This full-length portrait by Samuel Bell Waugh shows him aboard a ship, around 1839, as a newly appointed captain in his naval uniform. He entered the Navy around 16 years of age. He fought in the War of 1812 and in the war in Algiers in 1815, earning him the nickname "Fighting Bob." (Courtesy of Morven Collection.)

In 1823, Stockton met and married Harriet Maria Potter (1801–1862) of Charleston, South Carolina, the subject of this portrait by an unknown artist likely after Thomas Sully. She was the only daughter of wealthy merchant and plantation owner John Potter and his wife, Catherine. The Potters owned Colerain, a rice plantation outside of Savannah, Georgia, where they held over 300 people in bondage. Upon their marriage, Harriet and Robert received a sugar cane plantation in Glynn County, Georgia, on which they enslaved 108 people. The Potters followed their daughter to Princeton and built Prospect House (now part of Princeton University). The Potters were devout Episcopalians, and in August 1827, Stockton chaired a committee to raise funds for the construction of an Episcopal church in Princeton. Trinity Church was completed in 1833. Harriet and Robert had nine surviving children: Richard (born 1824), John Potter (1826), Catherine Elizabeth (1827), Mary (1830), Robert Field (1832), Harriet Maria (1834), Julia (1837), Caroline (1838), and Annis (1843). Harriet died at their Philadelphia home on Locust Street and is buried at Princeton Cemetery. (Courtesy of Morven Collection.)

This portrait of Robert Field Stockton was painted by Thomas Sully in 1851. Robert was born at Morven. After his mother, Mary Field Stockton, died in 1837, Robert moved back to Morven with his family. They had previously lived at Palmer House, just over a quarter mile to the northeast. With Princeton as a home base, Stockton's military and political activities took him to destinations across North America and overseas. In 1816, he sailed to Africa for the American Colonization Society to obtain the land that would become the nation of Liberia in 1821. He later became the president of the New Jersey Colonization Society. In Princeton, Stockton enslaved people including Hannibal Simpson, Kate, and Anthony. Around 1845, during active duty in Texas, he was appointed commodore of the Pacific Fleet. In addition to the Morven property, Stockton had land holdings in Virginia, Georgia, and the territory of California. On his Southern properties, he enslaved over 147 men, women, and children. (Courtesy of Morven Collection.)

Known today as Palmer House, this home stands at the corner of Nassau Street and Bayard Lane. It was built by Charles Steadman around 1823 for Robert Field Stockton and his young family. Stockton received this double lot as a wedding gift from his parents. Robert Field Stockton's strong family connections benefited him in political positions and business opportunities. (Courtesy of the Historical Society of Princeton.)

In 1828, Stockton partnered with the Stevens family of Hoboken to form the Joint Companies, which consolidated the Camden & Amboy Railroad and Delaware & Raritan Canal, effectively creating a monopoly on transportation in New Jersey. Stockton built today's Alexander Road through his Springdale Farm to connect the canal basin to downtown Princeton. This c. 1895 photograph shows the basin with the Branch Line crossing over it. (Courtesy of the Historical Society of Princeton.)

Richard Stockton Field (1803–1870) moved to Rose Cottage with his mother Abigail Stockton Field as a child. He attended Princeton University and practiced law. He commissioned John Notman to design a villa he called Fieldwood. The home, also known as Guernsey Hall, still stands on Lovers Lane. Field, the founding president of the New Jersey Horticultural Society, had impressive gardens and greenhouses, which became Marquand Park. (Courtesy of Mudd Manuscript Library, Princeton University.)

When Richard Stockton Field, nephew of Richard Stockton, the Duke, accepted the challenge of creating a law school at Princeton University, he paid for the construction of Ivy Hall on his own property. When the law school failed in 1854–1855, the building, designed by John Notman, became the offices of the Joint Companies. In 1871, Josephine Ward Thompson purchased the building for a women's library. (Courtesy of Princeton University Library.)

The steamship *Richard Stockton*, shown here in a pastel by William H. Rease from about 1854, was designed by Robert L. Stevens, president of the Camden & Amboy Railroad, and built in 1851 by the Harlan and Hollingsworth Co. The vessel was luxuriously furnished with extensive passenger accommodations. A closer look at the pastel reveals a horse and buggy on board. (Courtesy of Morven Collection. Gift of Liza and Schuyler Morehouse.)

In 1841, Robert Field Stockton and Swedish engineer John Ericsson collaborated on the first warship driven by a screw propeller, named the *Princeton*. Ericsson came at least twice to Morven to discuss designs. On February 28, 1844, the *Princeton* cruised down the Potomac River with 400 guests, including Pres. John Tyler. Depicted in this lithograph by N. Currier, the cannon onboard, named Peacemaker, exploded, killing six. (Courtesy of Joseph J. Felcone.)

This painting, attributed to Frank Childs, is the only known rear view of Morven before the 20th century. The extended East Wing, visible here, indicates that the painting was completed after that 1850s addition. The small washhouse still stands today. This painting descended in the family of Aaron Clayton, the Commodore's farm manager. (Courtesy of Morven Collection. Gift of Barbara Clayton Grahn Garretson in memory of her grandfather Henry P. Clayton.)

This engraving of Morven by Benson J. Lossing was published in the 1852 *Pictorial Field-Book of the Revolution*. The gable-roofed vestibule in front of the door of the West Wing may have been a temporary structure erected to shelter the doorway in cold weather. The small wooden building in front of the West Wing probably housed a pump. (Courtesy of Morven Archive.)

RES. OF R. STOCKTON PRINCETON
N.J.

Published in an 1865 edition of John Sanderson's *Biography of the Signers to the Declaration of Independence*, this illustration appears to have been based on Lossing's view. The only difference between them is that the windows of the east wing are shown with plain, flat lintels. The editor noted, "The house is in a fine state of preservation, and is highly prized by the family." (Courtesy of the Princeton University Library.)

Robert Field Stockton and his daughters go for a jaunt in the countryside in this c. 1860 painting by Henry Collins Bispham. The Commodore bred and raced Thoroughbred horses, often naming them after New Jersey counties: Bergen, Middlesex, Monmouth, and Passaic. Two others, named Morven and Mercer, were reputed to have been acquired from a stud belonging to King William IV of England. (Courtesy of Hugh and Louise Stockton Hyder-Darlington.)

John Potter Stockton (1826–1900), shown here in c. 1861, was the son of Robert Field and Harriet Maria Stockton. When the family came to live at Morven, he was around 11 years old. He returned to Morven with his bride, Sara, shortly after their marriage in 1845. Stockton served as the US minister to the Papal States, as a US senator, and as the attorney general of New Jersey. (Courtesy of the National Archives.)

Sara Marks Stockton (1829–1887), portrayed here by Thomas Sully, lived at Morven during the time of this 1847 portrait. Sara was a Jewish woman from New Orleans who married John Potter Stockton. The young family lived at Morven until June 1849, when they moved into the newly built 83 Stockton Street (known today as Lowrie House and the home of Princeton University presidents). (Courtesy of the Historical Society Princeton.)

This portrait by Thomas Sully depicts John Potter and Sara Marks Stockton's son, named Robert Field Stockton (1847–1891), his grandfather's namesake. He was born at Morven on January 5, 1847. Sully recorded this portrait as "Oldest son of John Potter Stockton. Full-length portrait of a child of three, mischievously upsetting a basket of flowers from a balustrade." (Courtesy of Morven Collection. Gift of the Francena T. Harrison Foundation Trust.)

After his wife's death in 1862, Robert Field Stockton lived with his daughter Harriet Maria (her mother's namesake) and his son Robert and his family. The Commodore, shown here in a c. 1860 daguerreotype, died suddenly from cholera in 1866. He left behind an outdated will that bequeathed everything to his pre-deceased wife and a considerable amount of debt, including two mortgages on Morven. (Courtesy of the Historical Society of Princeton.)

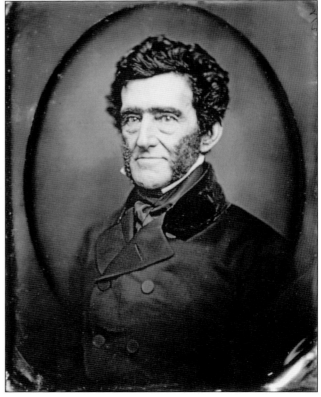

The house pictured here in 1920 was built at the behest of Robert Field Stockton for his son Richard. The house, designed by architect John Notman in 1851, is located at 86 Mercer Street. The property, known as Springdale, was part of several hundred acres owned by the Stockton family starting in the 1690s. Today, it is home to the Princeton Theological Seminary's presidents. (Courtesy of the Historical Society of Princeton.)

Another Stockton family house was at 58 Bayard Lane (the modern address is 15 Hodge Road). It was built for the Commodore's daughter, Catherine Stockton, and her husband, Rev. William Armstrong. Some similarities to Morven's central block are apparent. It is shown here around 1897 in preparation for Pres. Grover Cleveland to move in at the end of his term. He christened the home Westland. (Courtesy of the Historical Society of Princeton.)

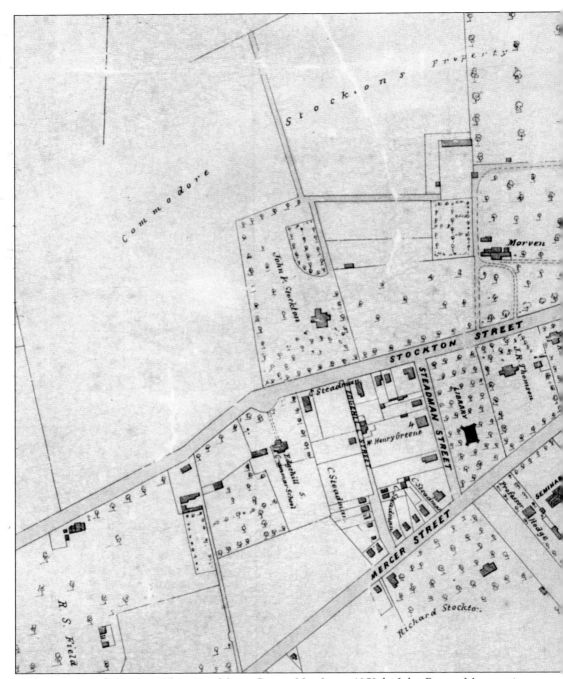

In this portion of *The Map of Princeton, Mercer County, New Jersey, 1852*, by John Bevan, Morven sits on a sizable tract of the land labeled as "Commodore Stockton's Property." The structure behind the West Wing is possibly a porch. Just behind that is the wash house. The Stocktons were flanked by their son John Potter Stockton to the west and by brother-in-law James Potter to the east. Across

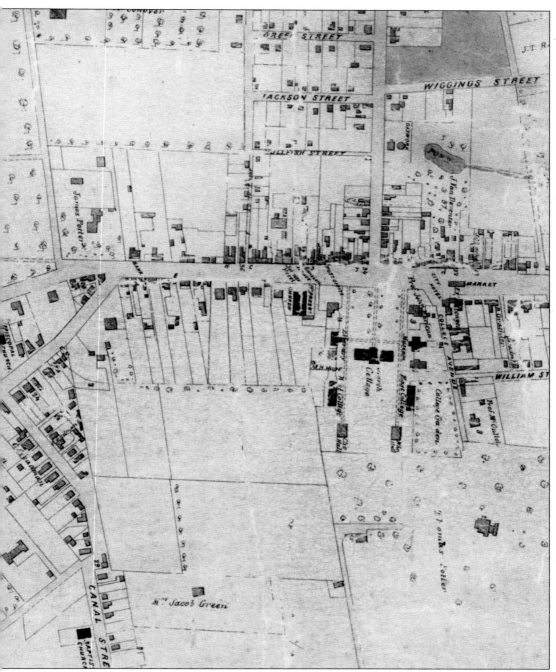

Stockton Street, the property marked "J.R. Thomson" was the home of the commodore's widowed brother-in-law. Beside Thomson is the property of Richard Stockton Field, the Commodore's first cousin. The Episcopal church, also across the street from Morven, is Trinity Church, which Robert Field Stockton and his in-laws financed. (Courtesy of Princeton University Library.)

Commodore Robert Field Stockton's building projects went beyond Princeton. He built a beach house in Sea Girt, New Jersey, on property he purchased in 1853. The borough takes its name from his estate. This 1885 photograph shows the property after developers added two large wings to the original house in the center to open as a hotel (first called Beach House and then Stockton Hotel). (Courtesy of the Library Company of Philadelphia.)

This grisaille drawing of Morven was done by Augustus G. Heaton in the 1870s. An engraved version was later published in John F. Hageman's *History of Princeton and Its Institutions*. While no portico is shown at the door to the east wing, there is a short flight of steps. (Courtesy of the Historical Society of Princeton.)

Four

SAMUEL WITHAM AND SARAH HODGE STOCKTON

Three years after Commodore Stockton's death, his nephew Samuel Witham Stockton (1834–1899) took ownership of Morven. This map of Princeton shows the property as it was in 1874. Visible toward the center-left, the Morven property stretches north, dotted with stables and outbuildings, including a greenhouse constructed during the 1850s. This was drawn by H.H. Bailey, lithographed by Breuker and Kessler, and published by Charles O. Hudnut. (Courtesy of Princeton University Library.)

Described by Alfred Hoyt Bill as "every inch a veteran cavalry officer, spare and wiry of figure, handsome in face with a drooping white mustache," Samuel Witham Stockton, in this painting by John Potter Cuyler (1867–1939), descended from Stocktons on both sides. His father, also Samuel Witham Stockton (1801–1836), was the brother of Commodore Stockton, and his mother, Mary Hunter Stockton Hodge (1808–1879), was Richard "the Duke" Stockton's niece. (Courtesy of the New Jersey State Museum, Museum Purchase, FA1991.24)

Just before leaving the Army in 1866, Samuel married his step-sister, Sarah Hodge (1840–1912). Born in New Jersey, she was the daughter of Charles Hodge, whom Samuel's mother, Mary, had married after becoming widowed. Sarah's great-great-grandfather was Benjamin Franklin. Sarah grew up in a family of theologians and was a member of the First Presbyterian Church in Princeton. (Courtesy of Hodge family photographs, Special Collections, Princeton Theological Seminary Libraries.)

Before acquiring Morven, Samuel purchased Hay Ridge Farm, located west of Elm Road. The site was later dubbed Constitution Hill, a name derived from the legend that the New Jersey Constitution was drafted there in 1776. Pictured here around 1890, it was demolished in 1896 to make way for the Jacobean mansion built by Junius Spencer Morgan that still stands today. (Courtesy of the Historical Society of Princeton.)

THE STOCKTON MANSION.

This view of Morven was featured in *Appleton's Journal* on December 25, 1875. The following year, Samuel Stockton served as the grand marshal of Princeton's centennial celebration of the nation's founding. The *Princeton Press* remembered Samuel as "greatly loved for his genial disposition, the sincerity of his affection, and the earnestness of his devotion to that which he regarded as right and true." (Courtesy of Making of America Journals.)

Samuel and Sarah had seven children: Charles, Richard, David, Mary, Sarah, Catherine, and Annis (not yet born at the time of this c. 1883 photograph). Posing on the front portico of Morven are, from left to right, (first row) Caspar Wistar Hodge Jr., Richard Stockton, Sarah B. Stockton, Charles Stockton, and Sarah B. Hodge; (second row) Mary Blanchard Hodge (in front of left column), Angelina Hodge (with hat), Caspar Wistar Hodge, Sarah Hodge Stockton holding daughter Katharine Wistar Stockton, Archibald Alexander Hodge holding nephew David Stockton, and Elizabeth H. Hodge; (third row) Margaret McLaren Woods Hodge, Mary Stockton (leaning on left column), Angelina Post Hodge holding daughter Sarah Madeline Hodge, Richard Harlan, Alice Adeline Post Scott holding son Charles Scott, and Mary Hodge Scott (?) (seated); (fourth row) John Aspinwall Hodge Jr., Richard Morse Hodge, and Samuel Witham Stockton. (Courtesy of Special Collections, Princeton Theological Seminary Library).

In this c. 1880 photograph, a "military troop" of Stockton children play encampment in Morven's orchard. "Major Sam," as he was known, was well liked by the children. In the winter, there was skating on the Morven pond and sledding along Elm Road. In the warmer months, boys and girls played baseball and football near the orchard along Bayard Lane. (Courtesy of Special Collections, Princeton Theological Seminary Library.)

This c. 1885 photograph of Samuel Witham Stockton and his family shows Morven's Dining Room. Samuel converted the East Wing to an apartment for brother-in-law Archibald Alexander Hodge's family, who stayed for a year. The rooms were then occupied by Samuel's widowed mother, Mary Hunter Stockton Hodge, and Sarah's widowed sister Mary Hodge Scott, her son William Berryman Scott (future Princeton geologist and paleontologist), William's wife, Alice, and their baby Charles. (Courtesy of Morven Archive.)

This c. 1892 photograph shows the north side of Morven's Dining Room. The two portraits above the fireplace by Christian Gullager are Rev. Andrew and Mary Hunter (grandparents of Samuel Witham Stockton). On Christmas day 1880, the Morven Dining Room saw 24 family members sit down to dinner. (Courtesy of Morven Archive.)

The bedchamber in this c. 1885 image is possibly the southwest bedroom. The patterned wallpaper is in less than pristine condition. A number of servants helped keep Morven running during this time. There was Julia Cox, 18, and Ellen Murphey, 45, both children of Irish immigrants, as well as Mary A. Grogan, who was Irish; Annie Hahn, 15, the daughter of German immigrants; and Katy Stout. (Courtesy of Morven Archive.)

William Berryman Scott (1858–1947) was a nephew to Sarah Hodge Stockton. Prior to this 1902 photograph by the Pach Brothers studio, he lived at Morven with his widowed mother, Mary Scott, his wife, Alice Post, and their young son. He graduated from Princeton University in 1877 and became a noted paleontologist and Princeton professor of geology. (Photograph by Pach Brothers, courtesy of Biblioteca di Geoscienze, Universita di Padova.)

Five

BAYARD AND
HELEN SHIELDS STOCKTON

Dr. Charles W. Shields (1825–1904), a Princeton University professor, purchased Morven to keep the home in the Stockton line. While Shields himself was not a Stockton, his daughter, Charlotte, had married Bayard Stockton, grandson of the Commodore. Shields wrote, "It is better that a Stockton should have the place than that Leigh, the butcher, should flourish in the seat of their ancestors." (Courtesy of Princeton University Library.)

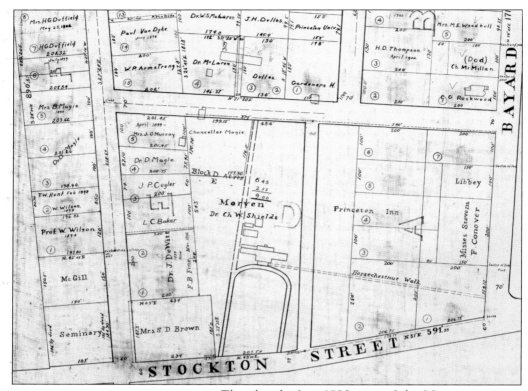

This detail of an 1890 map of the Morven property drawn by Ernest Sandoz shows the subdivisions made by Samuel Witham Stockton's trustees. When Dr. Shields purchased Morven in 1891, it sat on 11 acres. He immediately subdivided it and sold six acres on Bayard Lane to a group building the Princeton Inn. Notable neighbors include Prof. Woodrow Wilson on Library Place. (Courtesy of Special Collections, Princeton University Library.)

Charlotte Shields Stockton (1851–1891), seen here in 1868, was Dr. Shield's only child with his first wife, Charlotte Bain Shields. Charlotte's mother died when she was just a year old. Charlotte married Bayard Stockton in 1881 and had two surviving sons. By the time her father's purchase of Morven was complete, Charlotte had died. Three years later, Bayard married Charlotte's half-sister, Helen. (Courtesy of Morven Archive. Gifted in honor of Richard Stockton III.)

Bayard Stockton (1853–1928) attended Princeton University and became a lawyer like so many of his ancestors. He practiced in Trenton and was a state prosecutor for many years. When Morven came up for sale, Bayard Stockton and his family were living with his father-in-law and his wife's half-siblings at Springdale, where he was born. Springdale had been built by Bayard's grandfather, Commodore Stockton. (Courtesy of Stockton Family Historic Trust.)

Helen Hamilton Shields Stockton (1865–1949) is pictured here in Morven's garden with her Great Dane, Viking, in 1908. Helen's time at Morven coincides with the peak of Colonial Revival, a cultural movement between the 1870s and the 1920s that encompassed architectural, decorating, and gardening styles inspired by a romantic retelling of America's past. She spent decades restoring Morven, embellishing its history along the way. (Courtesy of Stockton Family Historic Trust.)

James Shields (1867–1929), known as Jamie, was Helen Stockton's brother. They were the children of Charles Shields and his second wife, Elizabeth Kane. Helen and Jamie had two other siblings, Jane, who died in childhood, and Thomas. Jamie lived with the Shields and Bayard, first at Springdale and then at Morven. (Courtesy of the Historical Society of Princeton.)

Bayard Jr. (1884–1912) and Richard III (1885–1944) were the two surviving sons of Charlotte and Bayard Stockton. The boys were six and seven years old respectively when their mother died. Helen, their aunt, became their stepmother. When Charles Shields died in 1904, he left Morven to his grandsons, with his daughter Helen holding a one-third share as a life estate. Helen outlived them both. (Courtesy of Stockton Family Historic Trust.)

This 1892 view shows what Morven looked like when Shields acquired it. Helen Stockton recorded, "Papa, Bayard and Jim went to Morven after lunch. They said it is in shocking condition and I must not go over for some time yet—I think poor Papa is really disappointed. Both he and Bayard say they cannot see how human beings could live in such a way." (Courtesy of Princeton University.)

This 1897 view shows the wisteria, planted by Samuel and Sarah Stockton, which still blooms every May on Morven's front portico. The second floor of the West Wing contained two bedrooms and a bathroom for domestics, and others slept on the third floor. Morven likely had additional staff working around the house and grounds who did not live on-site. (Courtesy of Princeton University Library.)

In 1881, Dr. Shields commissioned architect Richard Morris Hunt to build him a home in Newport, Rhode Island. Hunt, who would later design the Breakers for the Vanderbilts, designed a "cottage" in the Stick Style called Nethercliffe. Helen and Bayard Stockton married there in July 1894 "in the left drawing room . . . under a canopy of palms with garlands of roses and white peas," reported the *Fall River Globe*. (Courtesy of Ryerson and Burnham Archives, Art Institute of Chicago.)

Initially, Helen Stockton resisted Morven, writing "that having two houses neither could be lived in as I like, especially Newport [and] it seemed to put going abroad quite out of the question." The Stocktons traveled to Europe in 1905, 1913, and 1926. During World War I, they spent August 1917 in Newport, Rhode Island. (Courtesy of the Historical Society of Princeton.)

Following her initial reluctance toward Morven, Helen Stockton soon realized that to have a historic home that had been modernized and appropriately furnished was at the height of fashion. As heritage groups like Daughters of the American Revolution sprang up across America, Helen found herself in a historic house, in a historic town, and married to a descendant of a signer of the Declaration of Independence. (Courtesy of Princeton University.)

This photograph of Morven was likely taken shortly before 1879, when it was published in *The Princeton Book* as an illustration for the chapter on Morven written by future resident Bayard Stockton. Interested in his family lineage, Bayard Stockton was an early member of the Sons of the Revolution and served as the secretary of the Washington Headquarters Association of Rocky Hill. (Courtesy of the Historical Society of Princeton.)

This view of Morven's Parlor was included in the 1899 publication *More Colonial Homesteads*, by Marion Harland. This photograph shows the archway Helen Stockton added across from the staircase. Other changes included the elaboration of window and arched door surrounds with the addition of keystones. At this point, Morven did not yet have electricity. (Courtesy of Morven Archive.)

This later view of the Parlor shows the addition of chair rails and millwork above the mantelpiece. The wallpaper has been taken down and electric lamps have taken the place of gas fixtures in this 1927 photograph for *House Beautiful*. During this period, the household had numerous live-in servants, normally three to four at a time. All but two servants were immigrants from Ireland, England, and Austria. (Courtesy of Princeton University.)

Helen Stockton spent a lot of time considering wallpaper and fabrics. She recorded in her diary that yellow and white paper would be "very effective and will make the hall bright on a dull day." A closer look reveals a spinning wheel just through the archway—an ubiquitous decorative element in the Colonial Revival period. (Courtesy of Princeton University.)

Commodore Stockton's Victorian-era mantels were a thorn in Helen's side as she strived to recreate Annis's Colonial home. She eventually replaced at least three mantels in the house: the Morning Room, Dining Room (shown here), and the most eastern bedroom. While she purchased these mantels from dealers, she led her contemporaries to believe that she had discovered the original mantels in other homes and returned them to Morven. (Courtesy of Princeton University.)

Helen Stockton hosted anniversary celebrations at Morven whenever she could conceive of one. The biggest celebrations were those around what Helen incorrectly believed to be Morven's 200th anniversary in 1901. Helen loved pageantry and costumes and used her celebrations to bring history to life. She took every opportunity to put Morven on the map and enjoyed mythologizing the Stocktons and their prominent visitors. (Courtesy of the Historical Society of Princeton.)

In 1901, friends and family gathered in the Morven Parlor to celebrate Morven's "200th Christmas." Helen Stockton is seated in the front row on the left, and her father, Charles Woodruff Shields, sits at the center. Helen and Bayard Stockton incorrectly believed that Morven was built in 1701, the year that the Stockton family purchased land from William Penn. (Courtesy of the Historical Society of Princeton.)

The Princeton Battle Monument, which still stands just east of Morven, was unveiled on June 9, 1922. As president of the Princeton Battle Monument Association, Bayard Stockton hosted President and First Lady Harding for a luncheon afterward. Guests at the luncheon included two future residents of Morven: Robert Wood Johnson Jr. and Walter Edge. (Courtesy of Morven Archive.)

Nine-year-old Bayard Stockton III (great-great-great-great-grandson of Richard Stockton, the Signer) played a key part in the unveiling of the Princeton Battle Monument when he "raised the folds of the flag which was then hauled to the top," wrote Christian Gauss in "An Account of the Dedication of the Battle Monument" in *The Princeton Battle Monument*. (Courtesy of Morven Archive.)

This photograph was taken on the front porch of Morven on June 9, 1922, just after the dedication of the Princeton Battle Monument. The guest of honor, Pres. Warren G. Harding, stands in the front row amongst Helen and Bayard Stockton's grandchildren. Bayard Stockton III, who unveiled the monument, is in the first row, second from the right. Christian Gauss's report of the day mentions that "over the door of Morven hung the flag used by Commodore Robert F. Stockton, grandfather of Bayard Stockton, when he commanded the Battleship Princeton." A glimpse of the flag is visible at the far left side of the image. Bayard Stockton (second row, far left), along with Allan Marquand and Moses Taylor Pyne, was the driving force behind the monument by Frederick MacMonnies, which Bayard deemed "the finest Battle Monument in America, if not the world." (Courtesy of the Historical Society of Princeton.)

Helen Stockton's attempts at historic restoration extended beyond the house and onto the grounds. She spent years trying to recreate and convince others of what she believed to be Annis and Richard Stockton's garden. She presented her experience and conclusions at the second annual meeting of the Garden Club of America in 1914 in her published talk "A Quest for a Garden."

In 1901, Helen asked Rev. Henry Van Dyke for a verse to engrave on her new sundial. Still located at the center of Morven's garden, it reads, "Two hundred years of Morven I record, / Of Morven's house protected by the Lord: / And now I stand among old-fashioned flowers / To mark for Morven many sun-lit hours." Van Dyke, who was a neighbor, also wrote "Joyful, Joyful We Adore Thee." (Courtesy of Princeton University.)

In 1927, *House Beautiful* published "Two Hundred Years of Morven I Record," a feature on Morven by Katherine Gauss. This photograph shows Morven's wisteria in its full glory. Notice the additional trellises trailing it up to the second floor. When the Princeton Garden Club hosted a tour of the town's gardens in 1926, Morven's wisteria proved to be the site's chief attraction. (Courtesy of Morven Archive.)

Helen Stockton identified Morven's washhouse, seen here, as Morven's "slave quarters," a mischaracterization that persisted in Princeton into the 21st century thanks to the numerous articles Helen published during her lifetime. In 1916, the trellis seen here was replaced with the brick section visible today. The trellis was replicated on the other side of the brick courtyard during Morven's restoration. (Courtesy of the Historical Society of Princeton.)

Around 1916, Helen Hamilton Shields Stockton added the section of the brick wall that runs between the washhouse and the mansion. Bricks salvaged from the nearby University Hotel, which was demolished that year, were used to construct the new section. (Courtesy of Stockton Family Historic Trust.)

This photograph of Bayard Stockton and, most likely, his grandchildren shows the curved wall by Morven's carriage house. Helen and Bayard included their grandchildren and great nieces and nephews in their celebrations of Morven, even creating a silent film that featured them in historic tableaux in 1926. (Courtesy of Stockton Family Historic Trust.)

By the time of Bayard Stockton's death in May 1928, it had already become clear that he and Helen could no longer afford to live in and maintain Morven. By June, Helen and her stepson Richard had rented Morven, along with its furnishings, to Robert Wood Johnson Jr. Helen lived another 18 years, residing in the Peacock Inn, which still exists just northeast of Morven. (Courtesy of Stockton Family Historic Trust.)

While she left webs of myths for historians to unravel later, Helen Stockton ultimately protected Morven's future by selling it to Gov. Walter Edge and his wife, Camilla, with the understanding that the home remain the governor's mansion or a public historic site, securing its legacy as an important piece of American history. This postcard of Morven was published by Van Marter around 1909. (Courtesy of Princeton University.)

"Morven" Residence of Rich. Stockton signer of the Declaration of Indpendence 1776.

Six

MARGARET SHEA AND ROBERT WOOD JOHNSON JR.

Robert Wood Johnson Jr. and Margaret "Maggi" Shea made Morven their home after they married in Paris in 1930. Johnson rented the mansion from Helen Hamilton Stockton. Johnson chose Morven for its proximity to the Johnson & Johnson headquarters in New Brunswick and its historic prestige. Here, Maggi leans against a tree alongside the driveway in front of the house. (Courtesy of Morven Archive, Sheila Johnson Brutsch Collection.)

After separating from his first wife, Elizabeth Ross, in 1928, Robert Wood Johnson Jr. (1893–1968) took a flat in London. During a trip to Paris that spring, he fell in love with Maggi Shea (1902–1997), whom he had met in New York. After a short courtship, Johnson divorced Elizabeth and married Maggi. Here, the couple is sailing to Egypt on their honeymoon in 1930. (Courtesy of Morven Archive, Sheila Johnson Brutsch Collection.)

As Robert Wood Johnson Jr. grew his family's healthcare company into a vast international enterprise, he was recognized as a forward-thinking employer. Johnson & Johnson pioneered innovations in hospital management, medical science, and social responsibility. It also employed women. Johnson believed in the value of female employees, although they were paid less than their male counterparts. (Courtesy of Morven Archive, Sheila Johnson Brutsch Collection.)

Maggi Shea was a fashion model and dancer from Connecticut before she married Robert Wood Johnson Jr. Maggi was discovered in New York City when model scouts for French fashion designer Jean Patou saw her perform in the musical comedy *Good News*. Maggi moved to Paris shortly thereafter. During her modeling career, Maggi was photographed by fashion greats Cecil Beaton and Edward Steichen. She also wrote a column for *Vogue Paris*. It was in Paris that Maggi and Johnson began a whirlwind romance. This portrait, as well as a companion portrait of her fiancé, is dated 1929. (Both, courtesy of Morven Archive, Sheila Johnson Brutsch Collection.)

The Johnsons were great entertainers, hosting guests like movie star David Niven and composer Leopold Stokowski (husband of Johnson's sister Evangeline). Indeed, the Johnsons held small dinner parties two to three times a week, often inviting faculty from Princeton University to speak on topics that piqued Robert Wood Johnson Jr.'s interest. Robert is seen here in Morven's garden holding a family cat. (Courtesy of Morven Archive, Sheila Johnson Brutsch Collection.)

In 1934, Robert and Maggi Johnson brought their only daughter, Sheila, home to Morven. By all accounts, Robert was smitten with Sheila—often slipping into her nursery to talk to the infant for long periods of time. She recalls starting her day by visiting her father on the second floor as he dressed. The pair would then descend to the Dining Room for breakfast together. (Courtesy of Morven Archive, Sheila Johnson Brutsch Collection.)

This photograph shows young Sheila Johnson and her mother, Maggi Johnson, in Morven's Garden Room in 1935. Sheila recalled that her nanny, Caroline Hay, would have her bathed and dressed for her father's arrival from the office, and that the moment he returned, he would come to see her. Maggi often spent evenings playing the piano in the Parlor. (Courtesy of Morven Archive, Sheila Johnson Brutsch Collection.)

In this image, a young Sheila Johnson examines a stone lion on the driveway next to the front lawn. Morven's front porch is just out of view to the right. The pair of lions, which stood at Morven since at least Helen Stockton's time, have been recreated and relocated to the Colonial Revival garden. (Courtesy of Morven Archive, Sheila Johnson Brutsch Collection.)

In this photograph, Sheila Johnson plays on her rocking duck, with a baby doll looking on, in front of Morven. Note how the wisteria, which dates to Samuel Witham Stockton's time, climbs up the front porch and the West Wing portico. A trellis on the wall has since been removed, as well as the stone curb lining the brick piazza. (Courtesy of Morven Archive, Sheila Johnson Brutsch Collection.)

The Johnson family employed a staff of 14 to run the household at Morven. Most important to Sheila was her live-in nanny, Caroline Hay (1903–2001), whom she adored. Other staff included English-born Arthur C. Clarke, known as "Clarke," the head of the household staff; an Irish cook, Ellen; a Swedish cook, Christine Swanson; a Scottish chambermaid, Isabel McKinnon; and an Irish waitress, Mary Egan. (Courtesy of Morven Archive, Sheila Johnson Brutsch Collection.)

This photograph shows Robert Wood Johnson Jr. and Sheila Johnson along the paddock fence at Morven, which existed on the site of today's parking lot. The building in the background is an outbuilding belonging to 73 Library Place. It is still visible from the southwest corner of Morven's parking lot. (Courtesy of Morven Archive, Sheila Johnson Brutsch Collection.)

Robert Wood Johnson Jr.'s lease provided that the Stocktons pay for taxes, insurance, and structural repairs. Johnson was responsible for all other renovations and $5,000 worth of unspecified improvements. Helen Hamilton Stockton protected her gardens with a provision stating that Johnson could not change any plantings without permission. Here, Johnson sits by the garden wall with Sheila and one of their horses. (Courtesy of Morven Archive, Sheila Johnson Brutsch Collection.)

Robert Wood Johnson Jr. kept two hunters in the Morven stable: Vanity (seen in this photograph) and Wild Oats, whom he rode often. In 1956, Sheila Johnson commissioned an equestrian portrait of her father and Vanity done by Count René Bouët-Willaumez (1900–1979), a former *Vogue* illustrator and friend of Maggi Johnson. Robert belonged to and became the president of the nearby Stony Brook Hunt. (Courtesy of Morven Archive, Sheila Johnson Brutsch Collection.)

Sheila Johnson had a cantankerous pony of her own named Gee. Morven's carriage house served as stables and later as a garage. The carriage house and distinctive curved wall still survive. (Courtesy of Morven Archive, Sheila Johnson Brutsch Collection.)

Located 60 miles northwest of Santa Fe, New Mexico, Ghost Ranch became a destination for the wealthy during the 1930s. The Johnsons made their first trip there in 1934 (the same year as Georgia O'Keeffe). Enchanted by what they saw, they leased land near the ranch headquarters and built a two-story adobe, visible here behind Sheila on horseback. (Courtesy of Morven Archive, Sheila Johnson Brutsch Collection.)

Of their trips out west, Maggi Johnson recalled, "I learned to ride and rope cattle, and for my pictures we would go north to Colorado. I would photograph mountain sheep, goat, and cattle, and Bob would fish the mountain streams." This image shows Robert Wood Johnson Jr. pushing Maggi on a donkey during a game of burro baseball at Ghost Ranch. (Courtesy of Morven Archive, Sheila Johnson Brutsch Collection.)

In this photograph, Maggi Johnson's mother, Margaret Hinchey Shea, plays with her granddaughter, Sheila Johnson, in the shade next to the brick wall constructed during the 19th century. This series of scrapbook photographs shows Sheila playing on her Morven playground complete with swings, a slide, and climbing bars. Sheila enjoyed climbing trees and spent many days playing in the garden with toys, pets, family, friends, and nannies. Her mother, Maggi, likely took these pictures. She had a keen interest in photography and set up her own dark room in the Morven washhouse. (Both, courtesy of Morven Archive, Sheila Johnson Brutsch Collection.)

As war broke out overseas, the Johnsons limited their travel and made modernizing changes to the Morven property. The addition of the pool, pool house, and tennis court was completed by 1941. In this photograph, Sheila Johnson and her friend Jane Henderson play poolside as a cat wanders by. (Courtesy of Morven Archive, Sheila Johnson Brutsch Collection.)

Robert Wood Johnson Jr.'s lease, which he renewed in 1934 and again in 1939, stated that he could build tennis and squash courts. A clay tennis court was put in, and the night lights, still visible today, were added later. The pool house, tennis court, and carriage house are visible in this c. 1941 photograph of Maggi Johnson knitting. (Courtesy of Morven Archive, Sheila Johnson Brutsch Collection.)

Morven's third floor (pictured here) was converted into two bedrooms and a bathroom for Sheila Johnson and her nanny. In the wake of the Lindbergh kidnapping in Hopewell and the attempted kidnapping of Robert Wood Johnson Jr.'s niece just 18 days later, Johnson instructed Sheila's nanny to lock herself and Sheila into their third-floor suite at night. Sheila was never to be left alone. (Courtesy of Morven Archive, Sheila Johnson Brutsch Collection.)

In addition to Joffee, pictured here with Sheila Johnson on the front lawn in 1938, the Johnsons had a corgi named Barkus who met an untimely end in traffic on Stockton Street. Sheila remembers her father as an anglophile—because the queen had a corgi, the Johnsons did too. Barkus was replaced with a cat that Sheila named Eagle. (Courtesy of Morven Archive, Sheila Johnson Brutsch Collection.)

This photograph of Sheila Johnson on a fall day reveals the back of the Morven property. She stands along a path leading to the carriage house, visible to the right. To the left is the edge of the horse paddock, and in the background is the rear of 30 Boudinot Street. (Courtesy of Morven Archive, Sheila Johnson Brutsch Collection.)

Sheila Johnson's best friend Alice Byrd remembers how she and Sheila would share a piece of chewing gum when nanny Caroline Hay (pictured here with Sheila) was not looking. Sheila was well-behaved, and Caroline loved her, but Alice remembers Sheila pushing her into the pool on one occasion. (Courtesy of Morven Archive, Sheila Johnson Brutsch Collection.)

Robert Wood Johnson Jr. wrote *Try Reality, A Discussion of Hours, Wages and the Industrial Future*, the precursor to the more famous Johnson & Johnson credo, at Morven, most likely in the Library (seen here). Johnson firmly believed that businesses had responsibilities to society and that the more companies lived up to these responsibilities, the more successful and profitable they would be. (Courtesy of Morven Archive, Sheila Johnson Brutsch Collection.)

In this c. 1942 photograph, Maggi and Sheila Johnson pose with a doll on the pool house patio. The Johnson family only used these new additions briefly. By 1943, the family had moved out following Maggi's and Robert's divorce that summer. Robert remarried two weeks after the divorce, this time to Evelyne Buff (stage name "Evelyne Vernon"). (Courtesy of Morven Archive, Sheila Johnson Brutsch Collection.)

Seven

THE EDGE AND MEYNER FAMILIES

When Walter Edge was elected governor in 1943, New Jersey did not have an executive mansion. Driving through Princeton, the Edges stopped at Morven and inquired about its availability. They learned that Robert Wood Johnson Jr. would give up the rest of his lease. Pleased with the idea, Helen Stockton agreed to the sale, with the proviso that the home would always function as a governor's mansion or museum. (Courtesy of Morven Archive.)

Before entering politics, Walter Evans Edge (1873–1956) was an advertising and newspaper entrepreneur in Atlantic City. He served in the New Jersey Assembly and State Senate, where he authored the state's first worker compensation law and opposed Prohibition. Edge had the unusual distinction of serving two terms as governor 25 years apart. The Edge family moved into Morven on New Year's Day 1945. (Courtesy of Morven Archive.)

Along with the purchase of the house, First Lady Camilla Sewall Edge (1901–1972), seen here with Walter Edge in Morven's hall, acquired some of the Stockton furniture to help furnish it. In early 1951, Edge offered Morven to the state. His successor, Governor Driscoll, supported the gift (although he thought it would best be used as a museum). The Edges remained at Morven until 1954. (Courtesy of Morven Archive. Gift of Luke MacFadyen.)

The Edges' children were teenagers when the couple moved into Morven, but their daughter Mary Esther was married to John H. MacFadyen in the Solarium in May 1952. Here, Walter Edge awaits her as she descends the stairs on her wedding day. (Courtesy of Morven Archive. Gift of Luke MacFadyen.)

Mary Esther and John MacFadyen cut their wedding cake in Morven's Dining Room in 1952. Mary Esther, an artist who had studied in Paris, wore a rose-point veil given to her great-great-aunt by Empress Elizabeth of Austria. MacFadyen, a Princeton graduate, had recently won a Prix de Rome fellowship in architecture, and the newlyweds began their new life together in Rome. (Courtesy of Morven Archive. Gift of Luke MacFadyen.)

Walter Edge married twice; his first wife, with whom he had one son, died in 1907. In 1922, he married Camilla Loyal Ashe Sewall of Bath, Maine. They had a son and two daughters. This photograph shows Walter and Camilla with their son Loyall relaxing in the Morven Library on what appears to be Mary Esther's wedding day. (Courtesy of Morven Archive. Gift of Luke MacFadyen.)

This photograph taken of the display of Mary Esther and John MacFadyen's wedding gifts provides a glimpse into the interior of Morven's pool house. A large set of silver and crystal ensured the couple was ready to entertain. Note the decorative wood paneling, which was recreated in the building's 2011 restoration. (Courtesy of Morven Archive. Gift of Luke MacFadyen.)

This photograph of Camilla Edge (far right) with unidentified household staff from around 1950 was taken in Morven's kitchen. The glass-fronted upper cabinets probably date to Helen Stockton's day and seem similar to the existing cabinets between the Dining Room and hallway. The Edges' last official entertainment at Morven was a 200-person reception in honor of governor-elect Alfred Driscoll. (Courtesy of Morven Archive. Gift of Luke MacFadyen.)

The official transfer of Morven from the Edges to the state occurred in January 1954. In his autobiography, Walter Edge wrote, "Few things in my life have given me more satisfaction than the dedication of the Princeton Battlefield and the gift of Morven to the state." This photograph shows Governor Edge with his dog behind Morven. Visible is the Solarium, which was extended in 1947. (Courtesy of Morven Archive. Gift of Luke MacFadyen.)

When Gov. Robert Meyner took office in 1954, the future of Morven was uncertain. While the state had taken ownership of Morven, there was debate as to whether the home should serve as an executive mansion or a museum. A bipartisan committee eventually decided that the most appropriate use would be as an executive mansion. Here, Walter Edge gives Governor Meyner a tour of his future home. (Courtesy of Morven Archive.)

When Robert Meyner began his first term as governor in 1954, he was a bachelor. Young, tall, and handsome, the *Saturday Evening Post* called him "the Glamorous Governor of New Jersey." While Morven underwent renovation, Meyner lived between his home in Phillipsburg and a hotel in Trenton. Here, Walter Edge poses with Governor Meyner by Morven's sundial. Notice the third-floor additions, since removed, in the background. (Courtesy of Morven Archive.)

This photograph, probably taken in early spring 1955, shows Walter Edge and Governor Meyner by Morven's pool. Newspaper articles explain that the pool was kept empty that summer while renovations took place on the home. But Governor Meyner was quoted as saying he would allow children to use the outdoor pool the following summer if there were enough attendants. Meyner did make use of the tennis court during renovation. (Courtesy of Morven Archive.)

The contract for renovations to Morven went to architect Edgar I. Williams (brother of poet William Carlos Williams). Drawings dated 1956 show several large changes, including a new kitchen, pantry, and servants' hall across the back of the West Wing. The front of the West Wing would then house an entrance foyer and coat room. In this photograph, a new chandelier is installed in Morven's Library. (Courtesy of Morven Archive.)

As renovations moved forward, a subcommittee was formed to help furnish Morven as "an 18th-century country house as far as possible and practical," according to notes from the Governor's Committee on Morven. When an initial hope for donated antiques did not come to fruition, Edgar Williams turned to the interior decorating staff at the department store B. Altman and Company for new furnishings to accompany some existing antique pieces. This view shows the newly furnished solarium. (Courtesy of Morven Archive.)

In January 1957, Governor Meyner married Helen Day Stevenson (1929–1997) and brought her home to the newly renovated governor's mansion. In this photograph, he carries his bride over Morven's threshold. No stranger to politics, Helen had worked as a full-time staff person on the presidential campaign of her distant cousin Adlai Stevenson in 1956. Helen became a valuable campaigner during her husband's re-election effort that year. (Courtesy of Morven Archive.)

In this photograph, Helen Meyner poses with a portrait of Richard Stockton, the Duke, by Charles Lawrence, which had passed from Helen Stockton to Camilla Edge to the state. This painting with many others now make up the collection at Morven Museum & Garden. (Courtesy of Morven Archive.)

This press photograph from the spring of 1957 was titled "The Bride of Morven." Here, Helen Meyner is seen at the gate between the back of the mansion and the washhouse. While the gate no longer stands, the two brick columns dating to Helen Stockton's tenure still flank the entrance to Morven's back garden. (Courtesy of Morven Archive.)

While photographs like this portray Helen Meyner as the quintessential 1950s housewife, she served with the American Red Cross in Korea and Japan from 1950 to 1952. She had a career of her own, including two terms in the US House of Representatives from 1975 to 1979 representing New Jersey's 13th District. She was a supporter of the Equal Rights Amendment. (Courtesy of Morven Archive.)

This dog is likely one of the Meyners' two poodles: Fluffy and Schatzi. They also had a Norwegian elkhound named Buster. Helen Meyner told the press that "all three dogs were Democrats." The man holding the poodle in Morven's Solarium is identified as Bill Scholottig, the butler, in this press photograph by Alan W. Richards. (Courtesy of Morven Archive.)

This November 1957 press photograph is inscribed "Meyner's dog 'Buster' looking for 'Muttnik.'" Buster appears to be sitting on Morven's East Wing front portico, looking skyward for the recently launched Sputnik 2, which carried Laika, the first dog (and earthling) to orbit Earth. Dubbed "Muttnik" by the American press, she was not expected to survive and perished within hours of launch. (Courtesy of Morven Archive.)

This press photograph comes from Edward R. Murrow's radio show *Person to Person*, which featured the Meyners and aired on CBS in December 1957. In addition to radio, Governor Meyner had been quick to recognize the political power of television and was comfortable in front of cameras. Seated in the Library, this photograph reveals the built-in bookcases added by Walter and Camilla Edge and an ashtray. (Courtesy of Morven Archive.)

On a rainy January night in 1958, the inaugural ball was held at the Trenton Armory for 1,000 guests. Helen Meyner posed for photographers on Morven's staircase before leaving. The Associated Press described her inaugural gown as "gray chiffon over white taffeta. The neckline scooped, and the bodice and skirt inset were embroidered in black leafy swirls . . . she wore a rhinestone necklace and earrings and elbow-length white kid gloves." (Courtesy of Morven Archive.)

In April 1959, Fidel Castro, the new prime minister of Cuba, was invited to speak at Princeton University. His speech, entitled "The United States and the Revolutionary Spirit," was followed by a reception at Morven. Here, Castro shakes hands with Helen Meyner on the Morven staircase as Sen. Joseph Clark and Governor Meyner look on. The party was deemed a success, although cigar ash had to be cleaned from the carpet. (Courtesy of Morven Archive. Gift of Ted Crane.)

In September 1960, Governor Meyner welcomed Sen. John F. Kennedy to Morven for a rest between campaign stops in Trenton and New Brunswick. It was a heavy day of campaigning for Kennedy, addressing over 65,000 people in a seven-county swing through New Jersey. In August, Senator Kennedy announced that Governor Meyner would act as director of his campaign in New Jersey, saying that he was "extremely pleased that Governor Meyner has been willing to take on this role. New Jersey is a battleground State and one which I have every confidence the Democrats can win in November. I know that under the direction of Bob Meyner we will achieve that victory." This photograph shows Kennedy in Morven's driveway (the front porch visible in the background), surrounded by students from Miss Fine's upper school, who ran to greet him after seeing his motorcade from the field hockey field. (Courtesy of Julie Fulper Hardt, Morven Archive.)

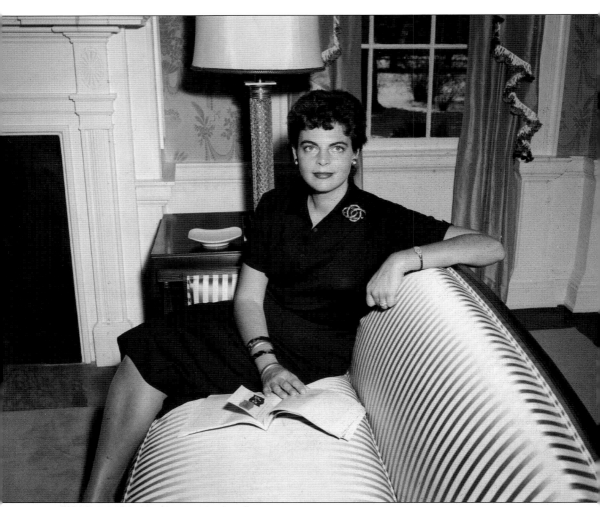

After her husband's term as governor, Helen Meyner worked as a columnist for the New Jersey *Star-Ledger* for seven years. Her column, In and Out of New Jersey, included stories about New Jersey residents, descriptions of her travels, and political commentary. She also hosted a talk show from 1965 to 1968 that aired in New Jersey and New York. She is seated here in Morven's Parlor, then called the Gold Room. During her own political career, Helen Meyner actively promoted women's rights and called for their greater involvement in politics. Upon her election in 1974, Helen said, "A woman's viewpoint is different, perhaps more intuitive and sensitive to people's needs in the special areas like daycare, environment and education." Remembering what it was like to be a politician's wife she recalled, "I was always on the back of the stage like most every other politician's wife. And I was always introduced as 'Bob Meyner's lovely wife, Helen' . . . I am still waiting, incidentally, for someone to introduce my husband and me as 'Helen Meyner and her lovely husband, Bob.'" (Courtesy of Morven Archive.)

Eight

THE HUGHES, CAHILL, AND BYRNE FAMILIES

Richard J. Hughes won the 1961 election, becoming the state's first Catholic governor. His confirmation as the Democratic Party's candidate took place at Morven. Hughes had been an assistant US attorney and a judge. In this photograph from February 1962, Richard receives a congratulatory telegram from Pres. John F. Kennedy. Seven of his children and wife Elizabeth "Betty" Hughes are seated around their family table in Trenton. (Courtesy of Morven Archive.)

Richard Hughes (1909–1992) and Betty Sullivan Murphy (1922–1981) were both widows with young children when they met on Halloween 1953 and were married the next year. With their marriage producing three children, the Hughes family consisted of ten children in total. Along the campaign trail, newspapers jokingly asked if the whole family could fit into Morven. They are pictured here in Morven's Library. (Courtesy of Morven Archive.)

Betty Hughes wrote a newspaper column called Memo from Morven and hosted her own television show from 1969 to 1974. She had a humorous and outgoing personality and enjoyed public life. Her mother, Helen Sullivan, also came to live with the family at Morven. Here, Betty puts away silver in the Dining Room. (Courtesy of Morven Archive.)

The Hughes family moved into Morven with their eight youngest children in March 1962. During the move, Betty was pregnant with the couple's 10th child. Of the move to Morven, Betty said, "If it can survive 261 years surely it can survive four years of the Hughes family." Here, they are on the front porch, dressed for Richard's inauguration. (Courtesy of Helen Hughes Patterson.)

Betty Hughes had a social secretary, Devey Chaffey, who is seen here in Morven's Dining Room with Hubert Humphrey. Betty said Devey could make a delicious lasagna, and the two had known each other since high school. A cook, Dorothy Jones, was employed at Morven. Additionally, Mrs. Randolph Eagan cooked with assistant Rovena Brown. Inmates from the state prison did the cleaning and gardening. (Courtesy of Helen Hughes Patterson.)

In this image, Betty Hughes and her children accept a set of *The Book of Knowledge* by Jack Hemphill in Morven's Library around 1962. Under the Hughes administration, higher education was expanded with the creation of the Board of Higher Education. The community college system started in 1967. Two state colleges, Trenton State College (now the College of New Jersey) and Ramapo State College were approved under his administration. (Courtesy of Morven Archive.)

As a family with many children, the Hugheses utilized the outdoor space of Morven for entertaining. The pool house and tennis court made a great spot to host a barbeque. This photograph was taken at Helen "Honey" Hughes's birthday party. The two women are Betty Hughes (left) and Clare McQuaid (right). (Photograph by Ace Alagna, courtesy of Helen Hughes Patterson.)

The mid-1960s marked a period of serious historic preservation in the Garden State. In 1964, New Jersey celebrated the tercentenary of its founding. The same year, documentary photographs of Morven were taken as part of a Historic American Buildings Survey (HABS). The two photographs on this page show exterior shots taken: one of the front of the building with stately flagpoles and one of the back of the building showing a screened-in porch on the back of the East Wing. Additionally, the New Jersey Historical Commission was established in 1966 under the Department of Education and still exists today. (Both, courtesy of the Library of Congress.)

The 1964 HABS project also documented some of Morven's interior. This view shows the Morning Room on the first floor, with a glimpse into the Library, which was used as an office. A painting of Mary Field Stockton hangs over the mantle. The floor is fully carpeted. As a public-facing space, the first-floor rooms tended to be the most formal. (Courtesy of the Library of Congress.)

On October 14, 1965, Coretta Scott King, wife of Martin Luther King Jr., performed a freedom concert at the Trenton War Memorial to raise money for the civil rights movement. First Lady Hughes and former First Lady Helen Meyner both chaired the event. Here, they are with Mrs. Wendell Price (second to left) and Louise Bayliss (right) at Morven in 1965. (Courtesy of Morven Archive.)

This photograph shows a rarely seen angle of Morven's Solarium (now called the Garden Room). The television was added as part of Betty Hughes's plans to make the room a playroom and children's area. Governor Hughes, seated, is talking on the phone. (Courtesy of Morven Archive.)

Another view of the Solarium, likely during the Hughes administration, shows that the room was carpeted. Betty Hughes also shared her plans to put in "heavy duty furniture" and bookshelves to make this room more family-friendly. Sports trophies lined the shelves among books and knick-knacks. Simpler drapery replaced the Meyners' toile. (Courtesy of Morven Archive.)

In 1965, Richard Hughes was reelected for a second term. This photograph, featuring Betty and youngest son Tom, ran in newspaper announcements that he had won. His term included events of national significance like the Newark Rebellion of 1967, a Cold War meeting for diplomacy in Glassboro, New Jersey, and observing South Vietnamese elections in 1967. In 1968, Richard became chairman of the Democratic Party's Equal Rights Committee. (Courtesy of Morven Archive.)

In 1966, the Hughes family took a month-long road trip to the Governor's Conference in Los Angeles. Betty Hughes said they put 5,550 miles on each of their two rented station wagons. This photograph shows the family preparing to depart from Morven. The Hughes family, from left to right, are Richard, Betty, Thomas (on tiger), Michael, Mary, Tim, John, Brian, Honey, and Patrick. (Courtesy of Morven Archive.)

As first lady, Betty Hughes hosted guests in a variety of locations. Pictured here from left to right are Betty, Lyudmila Gvishiani (daughter of Soviet premier Alexei Kosygin), Lady Bird Johnson, and her daughter Lynda Bird. During the meeting between President Johnson and Kosygin, known as the Glassboro Summit, these women and the Hughes children traveled by presidential helicopter to the governor's beach house. The last-minute event, which became known as the Seaside Summit, was organized in hours. (Courtesy of Morven Archive.)

Governor Hughes campaigned for Hubert Humphrey in the 1968 presidential election. Here, Hubert's wife, Muriel Buck Humphrey, attends a tented function at Morven in September 1968. Hughes was the standard bearer to the significant Democratic Convention in Chicago that year. He was also one of three candidates considered to be Humphrey's vice president. (Courtesy of Morven Archive.)

Richard Hughes tours Morven with former governor Robert Meyner. The two had known each other for many years through politics. They continued a professional relationship during Hughes's term as he appointed Meyner as chairman of the Commission to Study Meadowlands Development. (Courtesy of Morven Archive.)

The Hughes family resided at Morven until 1970, when Richard Hughes's second term ended. Hughes became the chief justice of the New Jersey Supreme Court. This photograph, dated November 7, 1969, was taken just after the election. Betty Hughes invited incoming First Lady Elizabeth "Betty" Myrtetus Cahill (1912–1991) for lunch and a tour of Morven. Betty and William T. Cahill (1912–1996) had eight children. (Courtesy of Morven Archive.)

William T. Cahill won the 1969 election for the Republican Party. The Cahills initially hoped that Drumthwacket might be renovated as the new governor's mansion, but the project proved too expensive. Instead, some interior decorating was done at Morven; the biggest expense was wall-to-wall carpeting. The Cahills moved into Morven in September 1970. (Courtesy of Morven Archive.)

Betty Cahill adjusts Christmas stockings on the mantle in the Morning Room in 1970. This was before the Delft tiles that had been painted black were uncovered. The Cahills were a more private family than the Hugheses and temporarily suspended weekly public tours of the home. They still had staff to assist the family, including a secretary to the first lady, Eleanor Wright. (Photograph by John Pietras, courtesy of Morven Archive.)

Betty Cahill shows Irene Daly Farley around the Dining Room in late November 1972. This was part of house tours that benefitted the Association of the New Jersey Neuro-Psychiatric Institute at Spellman. The cause was especially important to the family as their daughter Patricia suffered a brain injury from a 1969 automobile accident. (Courtesy of Morven Archive.)

This view shows the governor's beach house in Island Beach, New Jersey, as it was in 1973. The land had been purchased by the state in 1953. In the spring of 1970, the beach house underwent updated interior decorating at the same time as Morven. The Cahills, who had a shore house of their own, enjoyed summer visits to Island Beach. (Courtesy of Mary Elizabeth Cahill.)

Even if regularly scheduled public tours were not available, the Cahills continued to host many visitors. On this day in 1972, fifty descendants of signers of the Declaration of Independence received a tour of Morven. Here Henry Haines Stockton (left), a descendant of Richard Stockton, Roselyne de Viry Frelinghuysen, and Franklin B. Satterthwaite walk past the front porch of Morven. (Courtesy of Morven Archive.)

Betty Cahill and another woman adjust garland on the main staircase at Morven. Christmastime has always been an opportunity to showcase the historic home to guests. In a newspaper feature, Betty said, "Our greatest family tradition, of course, is that Christmas in our family is also a birthday," because daughter Kathleen was born on December 25. (Courtesy of Morven Archive.)

Four of the Cahill children lived at Morven full-time, and three others came home from school on weekends. William's mother and aunt also planned to move with them, as well as Betty's parents, Belford and Regina Myrtetus. Here are three of the senior family members around the Dining Room table. From left to right are William Cahill's aunt, Hannah O'Neill; Betty Cahill's mother, Regina Myrtetus; and William's mother, Rose Cahill. (Courtesy of Mary Elizabeth Cahill.)

Morven has long been host to multigenerational family gatherings. Here, Rose Cahill blows out birthday candles with help from her brother-in-law Charlie Cahill in the Dining Room. William T. Cahill watches with two of his grandchildren in his lap. Betty sits next to him in the foreground, and his daughter Teresa is behind William. (Courtesy of Mary Elizabeth Cahill.)

In 1971, Morven was designated a National Historic Landmark, shown in this postcard from around the same time. Gov. William T. Cahill only served one term. Cahill's term saw the creation of the Department of Environmental Protection, the luring of the Giants football team to the new Meadowlands sports complex, and the handling of a prison uprising in Rahway. (Courtesy of Morven Archive.)

In November 1973, Democrat Brendan T. Byrne (1924–2018) was elected governor, and the family moved into Morven in March 1974. This view of the Library shows it as it was during the Byrne family's residence. It is decorated with some caricature drawings of Byrne. Homey touches include records, a record player, and a game of Clue. (Courtesy of Barbara Byrne Stefan.)

First Lady Jean Featherly Byrne (1926–2015) sets out a vase of flowers on the Dining Room table. Jean grew up in West Orange and was educated at Bucknell College and New York University. She married Brendan Byrne in 1953. The couple had seven children, six of whom moved into Morven full-time. (Courtesy of Barbara Byrne Stefan.)

This view shows the Parlor during the Byrne family residence. Note the National Historic Landmark certificate resting on the mantle. The Byrnes referred to this as the "Gold Room." Some of the household staff included housekeepers Rovena Brown, Mary O'Hara, and Jean Gibbons. Rod ? and Bobby ? worked on the grounds. There was also a constant rotation of state troopers in the West Wing. (Courtesy of Barbara Byrne Stefan.)

This photograph shows Jean Byrne with her Labrador, Yankee, in the Parlor. Note the Christmas tree in the corner. The family also had a small mutt named Kipper, and after Kipper died, they acquired a puppy that bore a striking resemblance. They also had a cat named Cat. (Courtesy of Barbara Byrne Stefan.)

The governors-era kitchen is shown in working order. Two unidentified women appear at the back end. This photograph shows a freestanding island brought in to house more supplies in the long galley kitchen. Kitchen staff included Jim and Fran Masucci, who cooked for the family, and later Wavanie Mouko, Paula Hyman, and Rosemary Flanagan. (Courtesy of Barbara Byrne Stefan.)

The first African American athlete to win a title at Wimbledon and US Nationals, Althea Gibson (pictured here at Morven in 1974) broke the tennis color barrier. In 1975, Byrne appointed Gibson to be New Jersey's athletic commissioner. She was the first female to hold the title in the country. Governor Byrne, an avid tennis player, had Morven's tennis court resurfaced in 1974. (Courtesy of Morven Archive.)

Each governor hosted foreign diplomats. Here, Abba Eban, the foreign minister of Israel, visits Morven with Governor and First Lady Byrne in the Library in April 1975. In the aftermath of the 1973 Yom Kippur War, Eban was dispatched to the United States to meet with American leaders and improve the relationship between the two countries. (Courtesy of Morven Archive.)

Jean Byrne and her personal secretary, Petey Dorman (1904–2020), are pictured at work in the Morven Library. Sometimes during house tours, Petey dressed in 18th-century costume to welcome guests. She had former experience in a historic mansion, working for the White House Historical Association during Jacqueline Kennedy's restoration. At the time, former first ladies Meyner and Hughes both still lived in Princeton. Helen Meyner would even come over to play tennis. (Courtesy of Morven Archive.)

In 1975, Princess Grace Kelly came to visit Princeton with her husband, Prince Rainier of Monaco, to see potential colleges for their son. Here they are at Morven with their children Albert and Caroline. Later, the governor recounted the visit as a "disaster" because he served lobster; Kelly was allergic. Governor Byrne also knew Kelly's father, Jack, who owned an Atlantic City racetrack. (Courtesy of Morven Archive.)

In 1976, a nationwide celebration of America's Bicentennial took place. Queen Elizabeth and Prince Philip visited the United States and gifted signed photographs to Governor Byrne. Celebrations were held at Morven throughout the year, with a re-enactment of the march to George Washington's inauguration and special open houses. (Courtesy of Morven Archive.)

On October 12, 1981, the Rochambeau Bicentennial was held at Morven. Princeton was a stop along the route between Providence, Rhode Island, and Yorktown, Virginia. Members of the National Guard and six guides received guests at Morven. There was also a picnic luncheon hosted in Morven's garden. On January 18, 1982, the Byrne family moved out, and Morven ceased to be the state's executive mansion. (Courtesy of Morven Archive.)

Nine

RESTORATION AND MAKING A MUSEUM

Gov. Brendan Byrne and historian Constance Greiff stand in front of Morven in the fall of 1977. After the Byrne family moved out in 1982, the New Jersey Historical Society (NJHS) took ownership per an agreement with the state that it would raise $4 million toward repairing the building to use Morven as a central New Jersey branch. Under NJHS, Morven opened to the public on June 21, 1983. (Courtesy of Morven Archive.)

During this period, Morven was open for tours two days a week and for special events, thus meeting the requirement in Governor Edge's gift that the home serve as an executive mansion or museum. Here, costumed re-enactors take part in an encampment at Morven in about 1985, held as part of the Annual Richard Stockton Birthday Festival. Note the modern police standing guard at the gates. (Courtesy of Morven Archive.)

The costs of maintaining the Morven property proved too much for the NJHS. With the assistance of Alvin Felzenberg, New Jersey's assistant secretary of state, the New Jersey State Museum (NJSM) took over the operation of Morven officially on August 1, 1986. Here Felzenberg smiles behind Gov. Richard Hughes on the front porch at an event in about 1987. (Courtesy of Morven Archive.)

By the time the NJSM took over, Morven's gardens and buildings needed repair. In 1987, the site underwent a Historic American Building Survey (HABS). It detailed the floorplans of Morven. An earlier HABS report had been done in 1964 with interior and exterior photographs of the building. In this c. 1988 photograph, a person measures the icehouse door. (Courtesy of Morven Archive.)

A three-part research project also started in 1987. There was a documentary history from Constance Greiff, an architectural investigation by Peggy Albee, and an archaeological investigation done by the Historic Morven Research Staff, directed by Anne Yentsch. The first two items were completed in 1989. Here is a view of Morven as it was in 1988. (Courtesy of Morven Archive.)

In the late 1980s, before much of the exterior restoration, remnants of the building as a governor's mansion still existed. This 1988 photograph shows a fire escape that was installed during the Hughes administration. It reached the third floor, which housed children's bedrooms. It was removed in the summer of 1999. (Courtesy of Morven Archive.)

The archaeology of the site was much criticized by the public because it was perceived as destructive and messy. It also seemed to be taking longer than anyone thought it would. This c. 1988 photograph shows work being done in a trench dug in front of the mansion. (Courtesy of Morven Archive.)

Because of the negative public attitude toward the project, Gov. James Florio suddenly closed it down in January 1990. The trenches were filled in with assistance from staff members of the Department of Transportation in addition to prison laborers. There was no time or resources to complete a final report on the project. In this c. 1988 photograph, archaeologists work on a trench on the property. (Courtesy of Morven Archive.)

Historic Morven, Inc., a friends group that first formed in 1987, was revived in 1993. The group raised money to begin a successful three-phase restoration. Here are several key figures of the project; from left to right are project director Emily Croll, Secretary of State Carol Cronheim, director of the New Jersey State Museum Leah Sloshberg, and president of the board of trustees Georgie Schley. (Courtesy of Morven Archive.)

This view shows the central hall prior to interior restoration, with red carpet and a door to the Dining Room. The corners toward the front of the house are angled here, creating a hexagonal curve. At the far end, a small governors-era chandelier hangs from the ceiling. On opposing walls are an antique mirror purchased by First Lady Camilla Edge and a large portrait of Robert Field Stockton. (Courtesy of Morven Archive.)

A strong volunteer corps has always supported the public operations of Morven. Regardless of which entity had ownership, dedicated docents have welcomed visitors and interpreted history at Morven for decades. Here, in about 2000, two docents stand next to a fully dressed table in the Dining Room. (Courtesy of Morven Archive.)

In 1993, the decision was made to restore Morven to the mid-19th century because the most evidence of appearance existed from this period. This c. 1999 photograph shows the icehouse before restoration. The backboard of a governors-era basketball hoop is visible. The brick wall on the right side of the courtyard is the servants' hall, which was constructed by enclosing a service porch in the 1950s. (Courtesy of Morven Archive.)

Phase one of the restoration of Morven took place from 1999 to 2000. The phase was kicked off on June 17, 1999, with a celebration led by Gov. Christine Todd Whitman and Princeton mayor Mark Reed. Children from the Johnson Park school attended. Here, Whitman scrapes off some of the 23 layers of paint on the exterior of the building under the watchful eye of architect John Hatch. (Courtesy of Morven Archive.)

The c. 1955 kitchen and servants' hall were restored to an 1890s-era covered porch off the back of the West Wing. The removal of a rear center dormer and Solarium floor took place the same summer. Modern air-conditioning and heating ducts were installed in 2000. This picture, taken in August 1999, shows the demolition in progress. (Courtesy of Morven Archive.)

At the start of restoration, July 1999, Morven's exterior was still painted a creamy yellow with black shutters. By the end of June 2000, paint removal was complete and historic limewash was applied. Note the two mailboxes in front of the West Wing and the paved asphalt driveway, which was replaced with gravel shortly after. (Courtesy of Morven Archive.)

In this c. 1999 photograph, a man works on an interior brick wall of the West Wing. The opening just behind him is the main visitor entrance today. The floorboards and joists were removed in 1996 so that the area could be excavated. At the far end of the room is the original bake oven, which still stands. (Photograph by Thomas Gralish, courtesy of Morven Archive.)

A c. 2000 photograph of the tennis court from the north shows a net, floodlights for evening games, and a chain-link fence with a solid block in the middle, much of which were removed during the restoration. Behind it is the back of the 19th-century carriage house, and on the left side is a portion of the 1930s pool house patio. (Courtesy of Morven Archive.)

This 2000 photograph shows the beginnings of the replanted Colonial Revival garden behind the museum building. Two rows of newly purchased boxwoods were placed, and later on, a trellis was added back to the end of the pathway. (Courtesy of Morven Archive.)

Morven is mid-restoration in this picture from around June 2000. The front of the West Wing has been stripped down to the brick. The back porch that exists today is already completed, while scaffolding on the icehouse suggests work is being done on its exterior. (Courtesy of Morven Archive.)

In the late summer of 2000, a man applies paint to the front steps. Around the same time, the 1970s iron fence at the front of the property was removed and replaced with a reproduction of the 1850s fence. The fence was replaced again in the same style in 2023. In late September 2000, Morven celebrated the completion of the exterior restoration. (Photograph by Thomas Gralish, courtesy of Morven Archive.)

Horticulturist Pam Ruch tends to the Colonial Revival garden in about 2001. Visible are the young boxwood hedges that provide form to the garden. A new white trellis was built, modeled after the one visible in photographs of Helen Hamilton Shields Stockton's garden in the early 20th century. (Courtesy of Morven Archive.)

The next phase of the restoration started in 2002, mainly focusing on the interiors of the buildings. The original flooring in the West Wing was replaced, a new elevator was installed, and "non-historic" elements were removed (like closets). This work was monitored by Hunter Research, an archaeological firm. Here, a man works on a window seat near the stripped-down mantle of the Dining Room. (Photograph by Thomas Gralish, courtesy of Morven Collection.)

Here, an early board and supporters pose in the Parlor; from left to right are (first row) Ted Crane, Jane Burgio, Betty Wold Johnson, Georgie Schley, Carol Cronheim, and Leah Sloshberg (standing); (second row) Sheila Johnson Brutsch, Bob Bennett, Dorinda Hawkins, Emily Croll, Carol Rosenthal, Jackie Meisel, Peter Frelinghuysen, Sam Lambert, Carl Reimers, Ruth Wilson, Steve Jusick, and Austin Buck. (Courtesy of Morven Archive.)

Morven Museum & Garden had its grand opening on October 17, 2004. The festivities included re-enactors and a fife and drum company. Special events continued throughout the week with talks by historians and garden experts. The rooms in the mansion building, here in 2006, served as state-of-the-art galleries with changing exhibitions on the second floor. The washhouse became a gift shop with offices above. These functions still remain today. (Courtesy of Morven Archive.)

The 19th-century carriage house restoration was completed in 2009. It is pictured here prior to the work. Two later additions were removed, with one from the front (seen in this view) and the other from the back. Prior to phase one of the restoration, the front of the building was paved. It now serves as a gardening workspace. (Courtesy of Morven Archive.)

Restoring the pool house was part of phase three of restoration. Documentation and planning began in 2009. Interior and exterior repairs were completed in 2011. Later, in 2012, the iron fence was taken down, and the pool was replaced with the spray fountain. (Courtesy of Morven Archive.)

The newest building on Morven's site is the Stockton Education Center. Part of a long-term vision as part of phase three of restoration, it was completed in 2018. It serves as a much-expanded space for private and public events with space for staff offices. (Courtesy of Don Pearson Photographers, Inc.)

About Morven Museum & Garden

The Museum

Home of Richard Stockton, a signer of the Declaration of Independence, Robert Wood Johnson Jr., and five New Jersey governors, Morven showcases the rich cultural heritage of the Garden State through exhibitions, educational programs, and special events.

Our belief is that history is an anchor to the past and a beacon to the future. Preserving and examining the past is vital for educating good citizens who will build a greater society.

Our vision is that one day all citizens will know and understand America's history and pursue civic duty actively and responsibly.

Our mission is to preserve and celebrate Morven's legacy by sharing its authentic stories.

Exhibitions and Programming

Morven's second-floor galleries host changing exhibitions celebrating the rich cultural heritage of the Garden State. Our programs and special public events offer opportunities for all ages to explore diverse and interesting topics related to exhibitions and historical gardens. Our year-round programming includes both on-site and virtual offerings.

The Garden

On Morven's five acres, see landscapes and garden spaces, which evoke all of the historical periods, from the Revolution through the late-20th-century governor's residence. Come for a quiet stroll among majestic trees and lawns as well as seasonally changing flowers, herbs, and vegetables. Be sure not to miss our Demonstration Garden.

For more information and to plan a visit, please check our website at morven.org

DISCOVER THOUSANDS OF LOCAL HISTORY BOOKS FEATURING MILLIONS OF VINTAGE IMAGES

Arcadia Publishing, the leading local history publisher in the United States, is committed to making history accessible and meaningful through publishing books that celebrate and preserve the heritage of America's people and places.

Find more books like this at
www.arcadiapublishing.com

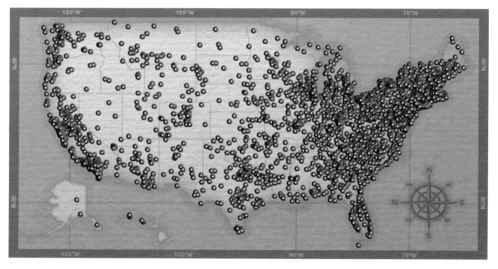

Search for your hometown history, your old stomping grounds, and even your favorite sports team.